The Power Of Man

The Power Of Man

Matrailvin Mosley

The Power Of Man
Matrailvin Mosley

Published by Spines
1500 Getaway Blvd, Boynton Beach, FL
ISBN: 979-8-89383-168-9

First off I would like to thank The Almighty GOD who gave me the insight and wisdom and love to write this book.
I want to thank my LORD and Savior JESUS CHRIST for the patience and strength HE'S shown me by The HOLY GHOST.
I would like to thank The HOLY GHOST for the words and compassion to say what was needed to be said at the appropriate time it needed to be said.
This book is dedicated to my love ones who have passed on and to the ones who are still present.
To my first wife Paula of 27 years who is now present with The LORD, thank you. Thank you for believing in me when I didn't believe in myself and thank you for loving me when I didn't think that there was anyone to love me the way that you loved me. You were truly a GODSEND to me. I could go on and on about us and about our love but that would take days. But know this that you were one of a kind and GOD blessed me when HE brought us together as husband and wife! Thank you and Thank GOD for you.
To Courtney and Mickayla my daughters, my girls. I am so blessed to be your father and hopefully someone you can call and rely on not only in times of distress but in life period. I love you both because when I see you, I see kindness, I see beauty, I see funny, I see intelligence, I see laughter, and I see lots of love thank you.
To my mother and father, thank you for loving me and thank you for being there in wisdom and in love and in patience thank you.
To my pastor Elder Larry Nichols Jr. and his mother Dr. Barbara Nichols, thank you for your love and wisdom , thank you for your friendship and guidance through this thing called life I love you and thank you.
To my wife to be Freddy. Thank you. When I see you I see

someone full of life and someone who wants to live a full life. Thank you for your patience and thank you for allowing me into your heart and into your life and thank you for agreeing to marry me and be my wife and thank you for still walking with me. I love you and Thank GOD for you and the love you give and show.

Contents

Foreword 9

1. The Power of Man 10
2. The Enemy Within 13
3. Walking in Forgiveness 17
4. Standing In The Gap 20
   The People Need An Intercessor!
5. Walking Upright Before God 23
6. Walking In Perfection 26
7. Walking In Your Calling 29
8. Walking In Greatness 32
   To Be Humble Before GOD
9. Get On Your Post 35
   Stay Watchful
10. Be Violent, But Don't Be Sinful 38
    Matthew 11:12
11. Lost And Found 41
12. Self Control 44
13. Problem Solver! 48
14. Whom The SON Sets Free! 51
15. Mark The Perfect Man, Walking IN The Footsteps Of JESUS 54

About the Author 57

Foreword

This book is for my brothers and sisters IN CHRIST whether it's a babe in CHRIST or a seasoned saint.

It's about knowing who you are and how to stand in this present and evil day. GOD is faithful and your Loving Heavenly FATHER wants you and I to be aware of the snares of the enemy and not to be caught off guard.

GOD wants you to know who you are and whose you are, to be strong and be courageous because you have a strong and courageous FATHER who will defend you at all costs!

Thank YOU Heavenly FATHER for giving me the right words in the right season for the right people! Thank YOU!

Now let's press on, there's work to be done before and after you start reading!

Amen and Amen!
IN JESUS Name Amen!

Chapter 1

The Power of Man

In the beginning, God gave Man the power to do what HE does except create. When GOD created Man in the garden, he was created from the very dust of the ground, but Man needed the Breath of GOD to live! Can you imagine the very first day of his living, Man seeing his Creator and Father smiling a pleasing smile of "it's good!" Now since Man (Adam) was created by GOD, it would be only fair that he had some of the attributes of his Father.

GOD gave Man complete dominion over the fish of the sea, the fowl of the air, and over the cattle and over all the Earth (Gen 1:26). It was only fitting since Man was created in the very image of an Almighty GOD.

Gen.1:27 reads, "So GOD created Man in HIS own image, in the image of GOD created HE him male and female created HE them." Verse 28, "And GOD blessed them, and GOD said unto them, 'Be fruitful and multiply, and replenish the Earth and subdue it, and have dominion over the fish of the sea, and over the foul of the air, and over every living thing that moveth upon the Earth.'"

GOD gave Man complete control over the Earth. But

GOD also gave Man rules and regulations that require obedience. Gen.2:15-17 reads "And the LORD GOD took the Man and put him into the Garden of Eden to dress it and to keep it. And the LORD GOD commanded the Man, saying, 'Of every tree of the garden thou mayest freely eat. But of the Tree of Knowledge of Good and Evil, thou shalt not eat of it for in the day that thou eat thereof thou shalt surely die.'"

If Man is to have dominion again, he has to learn to obey the voice of The LORD and not walk according to his own will. GOD gave all of us the power of choice or as some would say free will. Free will is a good and bad thing; it allows us to make good choices and bad choices. But it benefits you when that when you make a bad choice and realize it, you can repent and make a sound decision.

Back to the topic. This chapter is about the power that GOD gave Man. With this GOD-like power, the Man could talk to birds, and they would obey him. Man could speak to the fish and the whale, and they would hear him and immediately show up. Because Man spoke with GOD-like authority that was approved by GOD. Also, Man was in perfect fellowship and relationship with GOD. Man was in complete harmony with GOD, and GOD was pleased.

But, as always, the enemy was watching and hating the fellowship between GOD and Man, desiring some way to sever the relationship but, there was nothing the enemy could do, he was helpless. The enemy wants nothing good for you or your family and he loves when someone dies and goes to hell. Hell was not designed for you; Hell was designed by GOD for the devil and his followers (the fallen angels) because of the rebellion the devil and his fallen angels committed in Heaven (Read Revelations 12:7-9).

So, the devil in his complete rebellion and jealousy against you is determined to keep you as far away from

GOD as possible. Thank GOD for JESUS! The LORD JESUS who died a criminal's death and rose again to sit down at the Right Hand of the Father to give you and I back the authority that we lost so long ago in the Garden of Eden.

You see Man was lied to and tricked out of our spiritual inheritance and we were set up to fail. Again, thank GOD for JESUS who died and went to the cross so we could have that intimacy with GOD again through HIM (JESUS) (Read John 3:16). Now we need The HOLY GHOST THE Comforter to speak to us and the things of GOD! This is the GOD-power we need but, we need JESUS in order to get THE HOLY GHOST which is The SPIRIT OF GOD!

The power that was stolen from us is the power of our words. Your words have power. The BIBLE says that "Life and Death are in the power of the tongue." You can speak life or death to anything or situation, but you need THE HOLY GHOST if you are going to speak the correct things in righteousness. Some people speak the wrong things from their heart and with it comes curses, but with THE HOLY GHOST who will lead you in all truths and wisdom because HE is THE SPIRIT OF GOD will let you speak the appropriate things of GOD.

Chapter 2
The Enemy Within

The reason this chapter is called the enemy within is because the flesh (yours and mine) is our greatest opponent. And the enemy (the devil) likes it that way. Because his greatest strength against you is your very own flesh! It's been like that since the Garden of Eden because he knew that the only way to possibly stand a chance against Man (Adam) was the Man's wife (Eve). It wasn't a direct attack, but it came by way of the Man's love for his wife!

1 Peter 5:8 reads "Be sober, be vigilant, because your adversary the devil, as roaring lion, walks about seeking whom he may devour". Friends, the enemy is constantly watching you looking for a weakness in your flesh. Whether it's food, sex, gambling, lying, cheating, stealing, whatever it might be, he is watching you. The good news is so GOD. Hallelujah! We have a GOD and a SAVIOR who is watching us and watching the enemy. So, when our flesh acts up and becomes unruly, we have a HEAVENLY FATHER who gives us a way of escape.

1 Corinthians 10:13 reads "There hath no temptation taken you, but such as is common to man, but GOD is faithful, who will not suffer you to be tempted above that ye are able but will with the temptation also make a way of escape, that ye may be able to bear it." GOD knows all about your struggle, your strengths and weaknesses. When THE LORD JESUS was in the wilderness fasting for forty days and forty nights the enemy came trying to provoke HIS flesh. But THE LORD stood strong not relying on HIS flesh but stood on THE WORD of "It is written." Seeing how HE was THE WORD made flesh and when THE LORD stood strong HIS FATHER and HIS GOD backed HIM up.

Wow! Friends, when you stand in righteousness your HEAVENLY FATHER will back you up! Because HE made a way of escape for us, and HIS NAME is JESUS. Praise GOD for JESUS who not is not only our WAY-MAKER but our BRIDGE over troubled waters. Thank YOU, FATHER!

Friends let us not be deceived by the trickery of the enemy. But let us be watchful in all giving GLORY TO GOD. When I think of Brother Job how at what seem to be his lowest point, the enemy tried to get him to commit spiritual suicide through his wife by telling him to curse GOD and die. What an insult! Thank GOD that GOD knew what Job was made of and that he truly loved his HEAVENLY FATHER! Praise THE LORD! Friends, we all must be careful because the enemy tries to work through loved ones as well as your flesh. We're living in this life, so we still have work to do and there's a whole lot of fighting to be done.

Now for the ones GOD has called home, AMEN and thank GOD, you made it. Brother Paul says in The Book of Romans verse 7:18 it reads "For now that in me (that is my flesh) dwelleth no good thing, for to will is present with me, but how to perform that which is good I find not." In other words, I'm looking for something in my flesh that's good and it is not found. Your flesh is contrary to the Law of GOD. The Law of GOD instructs us not to covet things or people but, that is right up the alley of your flesh. The flesh loves to covet and it's what the enemy targets and he'll trick you into thinking that it's greater than what it truly is.

In the Book of 2nd Samuel 11:2 reads, "One morning David got up from his bed and walked around on the roof of the palace. From the roof he saw a woman bathing. The woman was very beautiful, and David sent someone to find out about her. They said she is Bathsheba, the daughter of Eliam and the wife of Uriah the Hittite. You see friends what started this thing off was David lusting or coveting another man's wife, which the Law of GOD prohibits."

The Book of Exodus 20:17 reads "Thou shalt not covet thy neighbor's wife, nor his manservant, nor his maidservant, nor his ox, nor his ass, nor anything that is thy neighbor's." Friends, you'll notice the second thing in that passage was about the wife and that is the first thing the enemy brought to David's attention, the wife of his neighbor Uriah the Hittite. Friends, you'll notice that whatever your flesh is desiring the enemy is going to magnify it. Sin opens your eyes to lust and whatever your flesh is desiring the enemy is going to blow it up and glorify it. It does not have to be sex, it can be drugs or alcohol, it can be gambling, or it could be violence. Whatever the time might be it could be anything. Remember, friends, your enemy does not sleep nor rest.

The BIBLE says in The Book of Isaiah 48:22, "There is no peace, saith the LORD, unto the wicked." So, friends, if the enemy is the wicked one then he has no rest nor peace. So, you have someone who is your adversary constantly watching you so he can get you to mess up and possibly make a mistake to end your life. But again, thank GOD for JESUS who came to give your life and it more abundantly.

FATHER, we bless and praise YOU and we thank YOU for YOUR loving SON, JESUS, LORD OF LORDS and KING OF KINGS.

Chapter 3
Walking in Forgiveness

When GOD has forgiven you, the power to forgive distorts the plan of the enemy. The enemy wants you to walk in unforgiveness. When unforgiveness is in your heart, it is hard to hear the Voice of THE LORD. Hearing from your Heavenly FATHER should be the goal of every child of God.

Remember, it is so important to forgive because GOD is waiting to forgive us when we mess up and make mistakes, which we do daily. Remember, THE LORD JESUS on the cross before HE gave up the ghost asked THE FATHER to forgive us.

The Book of Luke 23:34 reads "FATHER, forgive them for they know not what they do." Now if anyone had a right to be upset with people for persecuting, torturing, and crucifying HIM it's THE LORD. But THE LORD saw the big picture, and it was that the people needed a GOD who loved them and was ready to forgive them because HE was to show the love of a loving GOD.

THE LORD JESUS taught and showed us that how

can you say that you love GOD whom you have never seen but hate your brother that you see every day. 1st John reads "If a man say, I love GOD, and hates his brother, he is a liar, for that he loves not his brother whom he has seen, how can he love GOD whom he has not seen." Friends, love is a part of forgiveness. Again, we must learn to forgive one another if we are to have the love and power of GOD in our lives.

The enemy wants you to be hateful and powerless. But GOD wants you to be fruitful and multiply. Not just when it comes to your family and your finances but in every aspect of your life. GOD wants you to walk in victory not defeat. A victorious Christian is a forgiving Christian. A forgiving Christian is a person of power and authority. And when that happens the enemy can't stop you. Why? Because he doesn't have the authority to do so.

When Job's three friends came against him because they thought Job had sinned against GOD was the reason for all his misery he was facing had happened. So, GOD had Job to intercede for them because in HIS anger GOD wasn't going to hear their prayers. GOD who is wise and just wanted to forgive them because of all the accusations that they had accused Job of offended GOD and GOD was not pleased.

So, GOD had Job stand in the gap for them and pray for them because Job was innocent of all the things, he was accused of by them. In other words, his hands were clean. So, GOD had him stand in the gap for his friends. Also, Job had to forgive those same friends. Brothers and sisters, sometimes it's hard to forgive family and friends because those are the ones closest to you. Sometimes they'll bring up past mistakes, failures, and wrong choices that you made and those are the ones that hurt you the most.

JESUS had to forgive HIS family, and they are the ones that rejected HIM first. The Book of Mark 6:4 "But JESUS said unto them, a Prophet is not without honor but in his own country and among his own kin and in his own house." Again, The LORD was rejected by family, and by people who knew HIM yet when it was all said and done, HE forgave them showing THE FATHER'S Love.

Chapter 4
Standing In The Gap
The People Need An Intercessor!

Praise The LORD Brothers and sisters! GOD is truly Awesome! As we begin this chapter let's talk about interceding for the people.

An intercessor is one who stands in the gap between GOD and HIS people. Some would even say mediator. The Book of 1st Timothy 2:5 reads "For there is ONE Mediator between GOD and man, The MAN Christ JESUS." That is awesome! The LORD JESUS is still standing in the gap for us after all of these centuries! Again, that is awesome!

Brothers and sisters there are times in our lives that someone has to stand in the gap for you and I, be it on the job, at home with family wherever you may be. The Book of Isaiah 59:16 reads "And HE (GOD) saw that there was no man and wondered that there was no intercessor." GOD saw that the people were running amok doing what they wanted to do or thought what they wanted to do. There was no one to intercede on their behalf and therefore judgement was coming.

By the Holy SPIRIT, GOD was looking and is still

looking for people to stand in the hedge for the people. Yes, JESUS is our mediator, but HE also wants us to pray to THE FATHER in HIS NAME for the people as well as ourselves. This is a part of GOD'S Divine order of things.

The Book of Exodus 32:10-11 reads "Now therefore Let ME alone, that my wrath may wax hot against them, and that I may consume them, and I will make of you a great nation and Moses besought The LORD HIS GOD, and said LORD why does YOUR wrath wax hot against YOUR people, which YOU have brought forth out of the land of Egypt with a great and a mighty hand?" Amen!

Moses was willing to sacrifice his own life by standing in the gap for the people of GOD so that a HOLY GOD would not consume a not so holy people. Brothers and sisters GOD knows that we all have our share of flaws, but someone has to stand up and say for GOD I live and for GOD I die!

Sometimes you have to put your own goals on the back burner and say LORD, I come to YOU in the Name of JESUS as I stand in the gap for brother or sister so and so. Moses turned down a great honor of being a great nation so that a loving GOD in HIS wrath would not wipe out an ungrateful nation! Amen, LORD thank You!

There are people out there that are ungrateful about things in their lives, in their jobs, in their profession. Some are just lost and confused, and some don't have the right influence. Think about it you'll be ungrateful as well if you're around ungrateful people. Misery loves company. That is why GOD wants intercessors. HE wants you/us to come and talk to HIM about the condition our brothers and sisters are in. There are people out there praying for you. GOD knows people have prayed for me!

Make sure that when you stand in the gap for people

you ask GOD to forgive you of your faults as well. Sometimes we have make sure our garments are clean too! Praise THE LORD!

Chapter 5
Walking Upright Before God

What does it mean when you walk upright before GOD? Does it mean that you're perfect? No! Does it mean that all of your thought processes are pure? GOD knows the truth about it! Walking upright before GOD means that you have a relationship with the MOST HIGH and that there is intimacy there that cannot be shaken.

If you read the Book of Job the first chapter, it reads "There was a man in the Land of Uz, whose name was Job, and that was perfect and upright, and one that feared GOD and eschewed evil." Brothers and sisters Job was intimate with GOD because he had an active prayer life. Job and GOD were in constant communication with each other.

Chap.1 verse 5 reads "And it was so when the days of their feasting were gone about that Job sent and sanctified them (his children) and rose up early in the morning offered burnt offerings according to the number of them all, for Job said, it may be that my sons have sinned, and cursed GOD in their hearts. Thus, Job continually."

His prayer life was active. Now let's see what GOD said

about Job. Verse 8 reads "And THE LORD said unto Satan, Hast thou considered my servant Job, that there is none like him in the earth, a perfect and upright man, one that fears GOD and eschews evil?" GOD was bragging on Job. GOD was bragging on the fact that Job was upright. In fact, it is GOD that called Job upright. Friends, can GOD brag on you? Can GOD call you upright?

Moses was another man that GOD considered upright. GOD in fact said that there is no man as faithful in all is HIS house other than Moses. Wow! What an honor for the MOST HIGH to give HIS children! There are a host of men and women who walked upright before GOD!

Let's talk about David the shepherd boy who killed a giant and later became king of a whole nation. He wasn't perfect but he loved GOD! Or how Abraham who didn't know where he was going yet GOD led him by the hand to be the Father of many Nations though upon their first encounter, he had no children. And he too was not perfect.

Brothers and sisters when you come to GOD don't worry about being upright or being perfect just come to GOD and HE will perfect you and HE will make you upright! There are so many of GOD's children who have flaws and imperfections this list could go on for days and some even weeks. You just have to come to GOD through JESUS CHRIST our LORD and SAVIOR.

In fact, you will begin to walk in uprightness when you realize that you are not upright! The Bible says, "For all have sinned and come short of the Glory of GOD." (Romans 3:23) JESUS CHRIST was a man that walked upright before GOD. Some might say yeah but HE was GOD'S son. Yes, that is true, but HE was still a man and lived life as a man. HE rather please GOD and not other people and not please HIS flesh! And when it was all said and done GOD exalted HIM!

Philippians 2:19 reads" Wherefore GOD has highly exalted HIM and given HIM a name which is above every name!" Praise THE LORD! What a wonderful GOD we serve that will exalt you without you having to exalt yourself. Thank YOU, JESUS!

Chapter 6
Walking In Perfection

Praise The LORD, brothers and sisters! This chapter talks about walking in perfection. Perfection is not just a state of mind but a state of the heart! The Bible says that the heart is wicked above all things! The Book of Jeremiah chap. 17:9 reads, "The heart is deceitful above all things and desperately wicked, who can know it?" Friends, GOD knows the condition of the human heart and how it needs to be changed and how it needs to be perfect!

The Book of Genesis chap.17:1 reads, "And when Abram was ninety years old and nine, THE LORD appeared to Abram and said unto him, I AM THE Almighty GOD, walk before ME and be thou perfect." GOD knew Abram (Abraham) could not walk in perfection without HIM. GOD knew that this feat alone would be completely impossible. Though GOD told Abraham to walk before ME and be perfect, HE was basically telling him to walk with ME and I'LL make you perfect.

Friends, you can't walk with GOD without some of the attributes of GOD becoming part of your life. And one of those attributes is perfection. In The Book of Job Chap.1 verse 8, GOD called Job a perfect and upright man. GOD called Job that because HE knew that Job loved HIM. And Job knew that without GOD he was nothing. And realizing it he blessed GOD and in blessing GOD, GOD elevated Job to perfection!

JESUS CHRIST walked in perfection. Some of you might be saying well that's because HE'S THE SON OF GOD. True, JESUS is The SON OF GOD, but HE was also all man facing temptation every step of the way condemning sin in the very flesh that HE walked in. WOW, now that's impressive! Walking around in this sinful flesh and not a drop of sin on you! Glory to GOD IN THE HIGHEST!

Now here is the beauty of that, JESUS CHRIST died the wrongly accused death of a criminal and a sinner and yet was without sin. Rose again on the third day and then days later ascended into Heaven and then days after that sent THE HOLY SPIRIT so that upon receiving JESUS as LORD and Savior of your life, so that you can receive the HOLY SPIRIT and walk in perfection as HE did! Now that's great news!

Thank YOU, FATHER GOD you knew, that we can't do it without JESUS, we can't do it without THE HOLY SPIRIT! What an awesome GOD who had it all figured out from the very beginning of time! Oh, LORD thank YOU for loving us so! YOUR wisdom is beyond comprehension!

Now brothers and sisters if you want to walk in perfection call on The LORD JESUS and ask HIM into your heart. GOD knows you're not perfect and GOD knows that you cannot reach perfection without HIM! You can't do it no matter how hard you try. The Tower of Babel is a prime example of people trying to do things without GOD. Trying to get to where GOD is without GOD! That's insulting to an ALMIGHTY and all-knowing GOD (Genesis Chap.11 verse 1-9). You'll see their end results weren't exactly what they planned. But GOD was in full control all along and watching every step of the way. GOD is truly awesome!

Chapter 7
Walking In Your Calling

You might be saying to yourself, I don't have a calling, or I don't know what my calling is. Well, brothers and sisters, we all have a calling. It might not be to preach to a mass number of people, but you do have one. I can almost guarantee that you're probably walking in it and you don't even know it.

St. Peter was walking in his calling and didn't know it. The LORD JESUS told him that I'm going to make you a fisher of men. He couldn't see it right away but, wouldn't you know it on the Day Of Pentecost after The HOLY GHOST came, brother Peter preached a sermon of which three thousand souls were added to the Body Of CHRIST. Glory to GOD in the HIGHEST! Brother Peter went on to do great things for GOD (as you read the Book Of acts).

From the Old Testament you'll read how Joshua went from being Moses' minister to leading an entire generation into the Promised Land. Joshua was not the speaker Moses was, but he was a Griesel warrior who spent time with GOD and received his marching orders from the true Commander

In CHIEF. Joshua walked in his calling; he didn't try to be something or somebody he wasn't, but he stayed in his lane and walked in his position and achieved greatness. That is all GOD wants Us to do, stick with what HE has commanded us to do.

Brothers and sisters, it is easy to see someone doing something fantastic and want to emulate that person but, if GOD is not in it, and you try it and it doesn't go accordingly, then it's probably not the call you're supposed to walk in.

The Book of John 21:15, "So when they had dined, JESUS said to Simon Peter, Simon's son of Jonas, Lovest thou ME more than these? He said unto HIM, Yea LORD, thou knowest that I love thee. HE (JESUS) said unto him, feed my lambs. HE says unto him again the second time, Simon's son of Jonas Lovest thou ME? He said unto HIM, Yea LORD THOU knowest that I love thee. HE said unto him to feed my sheep. HE said unto him for the third time Simon son of Jonas Lovest thou me? Peter was grieved because HE said unto him the third time, Lovest thou me? And he said unto HIM, LORD thou knowest all things, thou know that I love thee. JESUS said unto him feed MY SHEEP. (Verse 21) Peter seeing him said unto JESUS, LORD and what shall this man do? JESUS said unto him what is that to thee? Follow ME (KJV)"

Bottom line, JESUS was telling Peter don't worry about anyone else just do what I told you to do! Friends, isn't that what THE LORD is telling all of US, stay in our own lane and walk OUT our own salvation with fear and trembling? Our calling is our calling, and we have to live it out and walk it out. Listen, we have a purpose and a call, what's yours?

GOD has placed greatness inside each of us and we should know it and if we don't know it, we have to seek the

Face of GOD to find it out, because GOD knows all and sees all and will reveal it to us as we take HIS Hand and walk. HE'LL show us step by step, we just have to trust and believe.

Chapter 8
Walking In Greatness
To Be Humble Before GOD

Praise The LORD, brothers and sisters! Everyone wants to be great! But everyone does not want to be humble. To be humble, one would have to acknowledge that there is someone or something greater than themselves! To us Christians, we acknowledge JESUS CHRIST (By our Heavenly FATHER) is greater than us. JESUS CHRIST even acknowledged that the Heavenly Father was greater than HIMSELF!

John 14:28 reads, "Ye have heard how I said unto you I go away and come again unto you. If you loved ME ye would rejoice, because I said I go unto The FATHER for MY FATHER is greater than I."

Greatness often comes with a price. If you want to be great, you not only have to be humble, but you must also be ready to suffer for it! Greatness is never given but it is often earned. People can heap praises of greatness on someone, but what did they do to earn it.

The Book of Hebrews 12:2 reads "Looking unto JESUS The Author and Finisher of Our Faith, who for the joy that set before HIM endured the Cross, despising the shame, and is set down at the Right Hand of The Throne Of GOD."

If you want to be great, be prepared to go through trials, tribulations, and obstacles. The enemy will try his best to put you through the ringer, and while he is doing that GOD will give you the strength to go through and endure whereas others would have died in the process. Since the beginning of creation, you and I were born to be great the moment GOD breathed into us the Breath Of LIFE.

Genesis 1:26 reads "And GOD said, Let US make man in OUR IMAGE after OUR LIKENESS, and let them have dominion over the fish of the sea, and the fowl of the air and over the cattle, and over all the Earth, and over every creeping thing that creepeth upon the Earth" Genesis 2:7 reads "And The LORD GOD formed man of the dust of the ground, and breathed into his nostrils the Breath Of LIFE, and man became a living soul."

WOW! Our Heavenly FATHER first made us in HIS IMAGE and then gave us dominion then HE breathed into us HIS very essence. Think about it saints we have the very attributes of GOD on the inside of us! Then HE went and gave us HIS HOLY SPIRIT now that's a sweet deal! But the deal was first made sweet when HE gave us HIS precious SON The LORD JESUS who went about showing The FATHER'S LOVE toward us and how much HE cares for us.

That is why the Heavenly FATHER wants us to walk in the footsteps of JESUS who was humble as a lamb but who walks with the boldness of a mighty king. That is why the enemy tries to oppress us so much because he knows what's inside of us, we just don't know it! The enemy wants you and I to be boastful, prideful, and vain. The very attributes that GOD despises.

It's one thing to be confident but it's another to be arrogant. If you want to be great and walk in greatness, be humble and let GOD exalt you. For HE sees everything that we do. I believe that there is a hall of fame of greatness in Heaven for the Heroes of Faith and for the ones who walked humbly before GOD as they walked this earth! First Peter 5:1 reads "Humble yourselves therefore under the Mighty Hand of GOD that HE may exalt you in due time."

And that is how you walk in greatness, let GOD exalt you. Philippians 2:9-11 reads "Wherefore GOD also hath highly exalted HIM and given HIM a name which is above every name. That at the Name of JESUS every knee should bow of things in Heaven and things in Earth and things under the Earth. That every tongue should confess that JESUS CHRIST Is LORD to the Glory of GOD The FATHER." And that, my friends and brothers and sisters in CHRIST, is how you become Great!

Chapter 9
Get On Your Post
Stay Watchful

Praise the LORD brothers and sisters and be encouraged GOD is a good GOD! Hallelujah! GOD has called for some of you/us to get back on our post and resume our position of watchmen.

You see some of us came down from our position to mingle with the ways of the world when we should have held our position as a good soldier dealing with the hardness. And for this because we have not been watchful, and the enemy has snuck into the camp leaving the people for an easy prey!

GOD is calling us back to our assigned positions that the people might be replenished and saved. The Book of Ezekiel chap. 3:18 reads "When I say unto the wicked, thou shalt surely die, and thou givest him no warning nor speakest to warn the wicked from his wicked ways to save his life, the same wicked man shall die in his iniquity, but his blood will I require at thine hand. Yet if thou warn the wicked, and he return not from his wickedness, nor from his wicked way, he shall die in his iniquity, but thou delivered thy soul." You see friends GOD takes no pleasure in the death of wicked people but, HE has more sympathy for them.

That is why just like Ezekiel we as watchmen are required to warn them of when their destruction is coming. GOD is saying to the wicked people, hey the way you're living is wrong and death is coming, turn around before it's too late. In other words, repent (which means to turn around) come to me I have something for you that's better for you than the way you're living.

That's why our job as the watchmen is to warn them. If we don't warn them as we're commanded to do and they die in their sin, it's our fault, because we didn't say anything. It's like seeing a child on the railroad tracks playing and we see a train coming and we hear it and see it, but the child is so busy playing that they're not paying attention and the train comes and wipes out the child and we sit and watch the whole thing.

Well, brothers and sisters GOD is that train and the tracks are the sin and iniquity of that child's life and their just playing unaware that destruction is heading their way. But you see it. And the horn and whistle blowing are GOD telling you, "Hey, I'm coming." Though they don't see or hear ME, but you do, say something and you're like nope serves them right they shouldn't be on the tracks in the first place.

And the GOD says to you this your fault if you would have said something they might have moved! Now GOD is saying if you warn the wicked and he doesn't turn or repent then it's his fault he was warned. Same scenario this time you tell the child and you plead with them, hey there's a train coming you might want to move it's not going to stop and like a rebellious child they continue playing and even scold you for interrupting their play time, then the train comes.

In GOD'S eyes your hands are clean, you gave them fair warning they just didn't heed to the warning that came their way. So, we as watchmen need to get back on our post, if we're not on our post we need to return to our first love who is JESUS CHRIST, the only begotten of the FATHER, Holy and Righteous is HE.

Friends let's get back to our post and stay there being ever watchful as our Heavenly FATHER is ever watchful of us all. Because regardless of the situation that train is coming and HE will be on time! Praise the LORD! JESUS is coming sooner than we think we have to get ready and stay ready! AMEN!

Chapter 10
Be Violent, But Don't Be Sinful
Matthew 11:12

Praise the LORD, brothers and sisters! We give GOD Glory and praise saying, LORD Thank YOU! I would like to start this chapter off with a quick prayer.

LORD, thank YOU for YOUR Grace and Mercy, and LORD, we bless YOU for YOUR kindness and YOUR loving care that YOU show us on a daily basis. We shall forever give YOU praise and honor In JESUS NAME, Amen and Amen!

Brothers and sisters, have you ever been so mad that you wanted to fight? So mad that you wanted to say ungodly things? So mad that you actually wanted to hurt someone, in particular, the one you were mad at? Well, that's what we have to do. We have to get so mad at the enemy that we have to be willing to fight! So mad that we have to speak! So mad that we want to hurt him! But we have to get mad in righteousness.

JESUS said in the Book of Matthew chapter 11 verse 12 "And from the days of John the Baptist until now The Kingdom of HEAVEN suffers violence and the violent take it by force." Brothers and sisters, you have to get so mad at the devil that you appear to be violent, but you have to stay out of sin! Now, that doesn't seem logical because whenever you would describe violence you would describe sin.

The BIBLE says to be angry but sin not. Ephesians 4:26-27 reads "Be angry but do not sin, do not let the sun go down on your anger and do not give room for the devil." In other words, don't be so angry that you have misplaced aggression to where you fall into error so that you would have regrets about your actions.

The LORD JESUS got angry, but HE did not sin, nor did HE allow HIMSELF to fall into sin. JESUS had a righteous indignation; HE had a right to be angry! Matthew 21:12-13 reads "And JESUS went into the Temple of GOD and cast out all of them that sold and brought in the temple, and overthrew the tables of the money changers, and the seats of them that sold doves. And said unto them, "It is written MY House shall be called a House of Prayer but, you have made it a den of thieves!" Again, The LORD had a right to be angry, but HE was without sin!

The enemy wants you to sin and be in sin and stay there, but The LORD wants you to be free. The LORD JESUS said that to whom The SON sets free is free indeed.

Brothers and sisters, you have to get so mad that you start talking to GOD about everything, in other words, you have to get so upset that you have to start binding and loosening to get back your peace, your inheritance, and your peace of mind.

The LORD JESUS said that the enemy comes to kill, steal, and destroy. Friends, you have to get so mad that you go and have a talk with your Heavenly FATHER to give you strength to receive back what the enemy has stolen from you! Friends, I encourage you by the Grace of an Almighty GOD, go and get your relationship back with GOD, go and claim your inheritance that GOD has for you, go and get your family back, and again go and get back your peace of mind that GOD has for you! It belongs to you because GOD said it was for you and JESUS died and rose again that you and I might be reconciled back to a Holy, Wonderful, and Awesome GOD! And In JESUS Name we receive it! Amen and Amen!

Chapter 11
Lost And Found

Praise the LORD, brothers and sisters, I would like to start this chapter off with a quick prayer. Glorious GOD, I thank YOU and bless YOU. YOU have been better to me than I have been to myself and for that I say Thank YOU. Thank YOU for sending me JESUS the Author and Finisher of our Faith. And thank YOU for sending me YOUR Wonderful and Divine HOLY SPIRIT. FATHER without YOU I am less than nothing but with YOU I am everything YOU need me to be and for that I say Thank YOU! Thank YOU for victory, for fellowship and for the strength to walk the walk of salvation and it's in JESUS Name I say Thank YOU and Amen!

Once again Praise the LORD and Thank GOD for JESUS! Now brothers and sisters the title of this chapter as you know is called Lost and Found! Wow! The reason for that is because so many of us are lost and we don't know that we're lost, and we need to be found. The reason that is, is because a lot of us are spiritually blind! Blinded by the darkness, deception, and the distraction of the enemy. But GOD forbid we should remain in this state. Again, Thank

GOD for JESUS whom GOD sent to liberate us from the darkness and to walk in HIS marvelous light! Praise the LORD!

GOD who sees all and knows all does not wish for us to remain in such turmoil. That very nature is against HIS perfect will for us. The Book of Luke chapter 15:10-32 tells us about the Prodigal Son who wasted his inheritance and repented and came back home and his father received him with open arms and brought him into the house and celebrated his return home being a son and not a stranger who does not understand his father's will!

Friends, GOD wants you to come home back to HIS loving embrace, back to HIS care and to have a relationship with HIM through our LORD and SAVIOR JESUS CHRIST. GOD wants to heal you, deliver you, and set you free. But HE can only do that when you accept JESUS as your LORD and SAVIOR!

So many people only want parts of GOD and reject JESUS. GOD'S perfect will for your life is acceptance of HIS SON JESUS! Because when you accept JESUS, you're telling GOD YOUR will be done!

John 3:16 describes GOD'S Love for you and I and how GOD desires the reconciliation between us and HIM! It's GOD'S love for us that HE sent us JESUS, it's GOD'S Love for us that HE gave us HIS HOLY SPIRIT! Wow! What more could we possibly ask for from a loving Heavenly FATHER!

So many times, GOD wants to comfort us and love on us and let us know that HE sees the hurt and the pain as well as the abuse and misunderstanding. GOD through our LORD and SAVIOR JESUS CHRIST wants to hold your hand as you walk through this thing called life.

In the last chapter of the Book of Matthew, The LORD JESUS made a promise to the disciples (Matthew 28:20) saying,"LO, I am with you always, even until the end of the world!" Wow! What a wonderful promise from a Wonderful SAVIOR. To know that no matter whatever I face in this life I won't face it alone, even when I feel my lowest, to know that I'm not alone is very encouraging.

What a wonderful GOD who sees me even in my lowest state, never stops loving me even when I'm not being the perfect child, HE wants to come and talk to me and forgive me and give me hope! What a wonderful GOD we serve! Thank YOU, JESUS! GOD never wants to shut you out; HE wants to love you more than you can possibly imagined.

In the (Book of Luke chapter 15:4-7) The Lord JESUS is explaining and teaching them that when a shepherd has lost his sheep and he goes and looks for it and when he finds his sheep he takes sheep and carries it back home and rejoices when he gets back home to his family and friends and tells about a lost sheep, his lost sheep that has been found! Wow! What a caring GOD that when you belong to HIM, and you are lost has enough love for you to come and find you!

Heavenly FATHER, we thank YOU for being so kind and merciful that even when we get in our feelings and emotions and allow ourselves to get distracted, lost and of course YOU come and find us! Hallelujah JESUS and Thank YOU GOD! Brothers and sisters, it's time to get excited about GOD and HIS Loving kindness that HE shows us on a daily basis and the grace and mercy that HE gives us for something we didn't work for. Something we receive every day and yet we've never labored for it. Thank YOU, Heavenly FATHER, Thank YOU!

Chapter 12
Self Control

Praise The LORD, brothers and sisters. This particular chapter is about self-control or in some Bibles it reads temperance, which means moderation or voluntary self-restraint.

A MOMENT OF PRAYER:

Heavenly FATHER, we thank YOU and Glorify YOU and we thank YOU for sending us JESUS our LORD and SAVIOR and soon coming KING, thank YOU, Heavenly FATHER for YOUR HOLY SPIRIT and YOUR Grace and Mercy, In JESUS NAME AMEN!

Again, brothers and sisters, Praise The LORD. And again, this chapter is about self-control or if you want to call it voluntary self-restraint.

The funny thing about this chapter is so many people don't want to talk about self-control even in The Body of CHRIST. The reason that is, is because even as a child of GOD we still feel as though, I do what I want when I want to do it. We still feel like if it's not physically hurting you or me what's the problem, I'm not feeling any pain and I'm not hurting you, everything is okay. The problem is though you're not hurting me or yourself you might be hurting GOD!

Galatians 5:23 says "Self-control or temperance is one of the fruits of the SPIRIT." How can The SPIRIT Of GOD flow through you and this not be exercised? Is it possible to say that if you don't exercise one you can't exercise any of them? Now, that's hard to say, only GOD knows. There might be a struggle somewhere that needs prayer. Glory to GOD!

You might be great in all of the other areas but when it comes down to a particular thing you have no self-control. Now that's when the Body of CHRIST should at this time pray for that brother or sister that is struggling in this area and the temptation seems to be unbearable. That is why we are the Body of CHRIST when a member of the Body is suffering or going through, we are to lift them up before GOD in prayer. And in doing so not only do we help that brother or sister, but GOD sees our need and helps us too! What a wonderful GOD we serve!

Listen, brothers and sisters, self-control is never an easy thing to withstand it takes time and prayer to an Almighty GOD who sees all and knows all! As always Thank GOD for JESUS who is our mediator and who stands in the gap and prays for us continually!

The LORD JESUS exercised self-control all of the time. Well, you might say yeah that's because HE'S The SON Of GOD. Well, that's true JESUS CHRIST is The SON Of GOD but, HE also walked in human flesh, but HIS flesh did not get the best of HIM! The LORD JESUS went through the same temptations as we do and prevailed! Glory to GOD in the HIGHEST!

The Book of Hebrews chapter 4:15 says the exact same

thing it reads "For we do not have a High Priest who is unable to empathize with our weakness, but we have one that has been tempted in every way, just as we are yet HE did not sin."

Wow! What a Wonderful GOD we serve whose SON our Great High Priest JESUS CHRIST, who had the same temptation as me but overcame HIS flesh to stand in the gap for me and prays for me when I'm going through. So, even when I fall, HE (JESUS) is there interceding for me asking our Heavenly FATHER for mercy on our behalf!

Now, that does not give us an excuse to sin, but it should open our eyes to not sin at all. Sin is a broken law against GOD, that is why our Heavenly FATHER sent The LORD JESUS to us so that we can no longer be law breakers but that we can be reconciled back to a Holy GOD. That's how much our Heavenly FATHER loves us, HE sent HIS only SON to help save us from the world, the flesh and the devil.

GOD is constantly showing us how much HE truly cares but, with the lack of self-control we can't see it. It's like you have the lights in your house and all the lights in your house are off, you know where everything is, but you can't find the light switch. The same thing about lack of self-control, you know that's not right, but you can't find the light switch to see what's wrong. The lack of self-control will blind you and have you walking in darkness! GOD forbid that should happen to any of us!

That is why The LORD JESUS had self-control, though the world around HIM was dark and tempting HE constantly walked in the Light of HIS Heavenly FATHER! JESUS had self-control because HE had a very active prayer life, walking in The SPIRIT and not fulfilling the lust of the flesh! Galatians 5:16 says, "Live by The SPIRIT and you will certainly not gratify the desire of the flesh."

Wow! The LORD JESUS is still our perfect example for all eternity! Thank YOU, Heavenly FATHER! Thank you, LORD JESUS! Thank YOU, HOLY SPIRIT! What a wonderful GOD we serve! Amen and Amen! Thank YOU, LORD.

Chapter 13
Problem Solver!

Praise The LORD brothers and sisters, in this chapter we'll be discussing about our problem solver whose name is JESUS CHRIST! JESUS CHRIST the same today, yesterday, and forever is still solving problems no matter how large or small. As we live and breathe problems will come and it doesn't matter what time in your life it happens, they will come. 1 Kings 3:23-28 (read).

As you read the text, you'll see that King Solomon had a problem and by the wisdom of the HOLY SPIRIT he was able to render righteous judgement! Again, brothers and sisters' problems will come.

The Book of Luke chapter 9:10-17 (read) you'll see THE LORD had a problem because there were so many people to feed with very little food to get it done. But HE looked toward Heaven and blessed the food and then HE began passing out the food as HE broke it. What a wonderful Savior we have who is our perfect example and showed us that no matter how big the problem is our GOD is bigger than that! Hallelujah to The LAMB OF

GOD! Praise be The Name OF JESUS! LORD, we thank YOU!

You see brothers and sisters GOD is always bigger than our problems. The reason our problem is so big is, it's either our first time in the situation or we forget who our Heavenly FATHER truly is. Or sometimes it's a combination of everything from lack of faith to trusting GOD completely! When the Children of Israel came to the Red Sea they had a problem, Moses had a problem! How were they going to get over it? Exodus 14:10-25 (read) you see brothers and sisters as you walk with The LORD some problems GOD will lead you to so that you can't rely on no ones' strength but HIS and then there are some problems and situations, we get in ourselves!

Either way JESUS is our problem solver, ready in an instant to bail us out of trouble again, that we get ourselves into. GOD always wants us to rely on HIM because HE is seeking intimacy with us. GOD not only wants to be our Heavenly FATHER but our friend.

The Book of Proverbs 18:24 (read) says just that, that GOD is a friend that sticks closer than a brother! WOW! What a wonderful thought, that The Creator of the entire universe and the entire human race wants to be my friend! The LORD JESUS said that HE would never leave us nor forsake us. The Book of Matthew 28:20 (read).

So, we have a GOD, a LORD and SAVIOR who no matter the situation walks with us and desires complete fellowship with us. Now some friends will walk out on you for whatever reason but not GOD, GOD is saying I have you and no one can take you from ME and I'm not leaving you! In some situations, our friends will say every man for himself, but GOD doesn't do that HE'S with us through thick and thin.

If you read the Book of Daniel, chapter 3 (read) you'll

see the three Hebrew boys get thrown into the fiery furnace. You'll say brother, that doesn't sound like a happy ending when you start that story but if you keep reading, you'll find out that they had a problem, and The LORD was with them in the midst of their fiery problem and delivered them!

Again, I say Hallelujah to GOD In The HIGHEST! Praise YOUR Name JESUS! No matter the problem we have a problem solver by the Name of JESUS saying no matter how hot it gets I'M not leaving you but instead I'LL walk with you and live in you! WOW! What a wonderful promise from a wonderful SAVIOR! Thank YOU, Heavenly FATHER and Thank YOU for JESUS and YOUR Wonderful HOLY SPIRIT! Amen!

Chapter 14
Whom The SON Sets Free!

Praise The LORD brothers and sisters! In this chapter, we'll be discussing the true freedom that only JESUS can provide. The Book of John 8:36 reads, "If the SON therefore shall make you free, ye are free indeed." The LORD JESUS is not just talking about physical freedom but also spiritual and mental freedom.

Because when you look at it, so many souls are being held captive mentally and spiritually. People are being bound and enslaved in their minds and in their spirits. But Glory Be TO GOD in the HIGHEST, we have a SAVIOR who came to set the captives free! This SAVIOR's Name is JESUS, who died and rose again to make our freedom legitimate!

So many people get caught up with the cares of this world which enslaves them. Sometimes it's drugs and alcohol, sometimes it's perversions, or it could be something so simple like the trials and tribulations of everyday life. But the good gospel news is that JESUS paid the price in full on the cross! WOW, our Heavenly FATHER thought of everything.

When man first sinned in the Garden OF Eden, GOD knew that sin would not only separate us from HIM, but it would enslave us as well. It's only through JESUS CHRIST that we can have complete freedom!

Some people will tell you, "I'm fine, I'm free," and some will tell you, "I know JESUS," but they are still enslaved because there is no relationship. JESUS came to set you free because HE desires a relationship between you and HIM. Because a relationship with The SON is going to give you a relationship with the FATHER.

JESUS came to set you free because HE is the Bridge between us and our Heavenly FATHER to set us free from the devilish desires of this world! When you have a relationship with The SON OF GOD JESUS and you are drawn to HIM by the HOLY SPIRIT, your Heavenly FATHER will be drawn to you by the same HOLY SPIRIT! WOW! My Heavenly FATHER wants to commune with me!

So many times, I myself feel unworthy because I see me, and the me I see from a Christian standpoint is at times not very Christian. But Thanks be to GOD who reminds me that I will never leave you nor forsake you. Again, WOW! Because when I'm not being faithful, my Heavenly FATHER is always faithful.

Listen, brothers and sisters, this is a daily walk. You're not always going to hit the mark all of the time but that is no excuse not to be faithful and not to walk in the freedom that The LORD provides. Don't let the enemy get to you and try to remind you of your past and your past failures and your past enslavement.

When you allow JESUS to truly set you free, you're not going to want to go back and be a slave to sin and that sinful past. JESUS is not going to make you choose HIM, but The HOLY SPIRIT will lead you to choose HIM. There is a difference between being a servant and being a slave. A servant serves, a slave is forced to serve and normally against his or her will.

With a servant, their servitude is tolerable and there is not so much cruelty, with a slave, you're working against your will and the taskmaster is harsh with no sympathy. The LORD JESUS came that you might have life and life more abundantly.

The Book OF John chapter 10:10 (read) Freedom in JESUS is an abundant life regardless of the things that you have (because we all like nice things) it's all worthless without the freedom of CHRIST.

Freedom in JESUS means you can talk to HIM any time day or night HE'S not so busy that HE can't take your call. You just have to try and see.

Psalm 34:5 reads "Taste and see that The LORD is good." Brothers and sisters, the only way to do that is to try for yourself. Don't just take my word for it, open your Bible and begin reading and ask GOD where you should start.

I would suggest the beginning, but maybe GOD wants you in the middle, I don't know, ask and find out because only GOD knows! Praise The LORD and Thank GOD for your reading!

Chapter 15
Mark The Perfect Man, Walking IN The Footsteps Of JESUS

Praise The LORD, brothers and sisters rejoice in The LORD and again I say rejoice! Hallelujah! Let's start with a quick prayer. Heavenly FATHER, we thank YOU for JESUS and we thank YOU for the many blessings that YOU have stored for us, and we also thank YOU for the right now blessings that YOU have for us, and we bless YOU and thank YOU again, now FATHER guide us and keep us IN JESUS Name Amen! Praise The LORD!

This chapter talks about marking the perfect man and that MAN is JESUS. The Book of Psalms 37:37 reads "Mark the perfect and behold the upright for the end of that man is peace." King David prophesying by The HOLY SPIRIT is talking about JESUS. Now some of you might be saying that when JESUS was crucified on the cross that, that was not peaceful but violent and cruel. Yes, you're right it was those things, but that was not the end of JESUS. Don't forget we serve a risen SAVIOR who sits at GOD'S Right Hand in complete peace!

Some of you might be saying how can we walk in the footsteps of JESUS, after all HE is perfect? You're absolutely right JESUS is perfect and that is hard to do, but that is why GOD gave us HIS HOLY SPIRIT! Because naturally this is very difficult to accomplish. People would often use the phrase what would JESUS do? Well, I know for a fact that JESUS would not do anything unless The HOLY GHOST led the way. Even though JESUS was GOD'S SON HE was still all man. And being a man, HE needed direction from The HOLY SPIRIT even though HE was filled with The HOLY SPIRIT!

So again, people use the phrase what would JESUS do when these same people don't fast and pray, and they don't commune with The HOLY SPIRIT. Now this is not about throwing stones or talking down on anyone this is simply saying that JESUS was SPIRIT Filled and SPIRIT Led. Well, you're saying how can we follow JESUS if we don't have HIS HOLY SPIRIT? The answer is you can't! You have to have The HOLY GHOST if you're going to follow JESUS for real! Following JESUS and walking in HIS Footsteps is not an easy task. For some it's downright difficult.

Again, that's why you need The HOLY SPIRIT. JESUS said that The HOLY SPIRIT will lead you in all truth. (John 16:13) When JESUS told the disciples to follow ME, HE wasn't just talking physically, but spiritually.

To truly follow JESUS, you have to be filled with The SPIRIT and be led by the SPIRIT. That is the only way you can walk in the footsteps of JESUS. I mean after all what would JESUS do? I think HE would say let's get moving!

About the Author

My name is Matrailvin (Matt) Mosley and I'm an ordained minister and my call is to bring a sense of awareness to The Body of Christ, in other words to wake up the people out of their slumber.
Preaching The Gospel of JESUS CHRIST allows me to do that whenever and wherever my Heavenly Father sees fit.
This book, which My Heavenly Father has allowed me to write is about your everyday life and how you and I can walk it out no what we face in our everyday life or life situations.

www.ingramcontent.com/pod-product-compliance
Lightning Source LLC
La Vergne TN
LVHW010506160826
845677LV00012B/2683

* 9 7 9 8 8 9 3 8 3 1 6 8 9 *